LIFE BY
Design

52 Lists, Questions,
and Inspirations for
FINDING YOUR HAPPINESS

MIRANDA HERSEY

CASTLE POINT BOOKS
NEW YORK

TABLE OF CONTENTS

INTRODUCTION

WHEREVER YOU ARE, YOU'RE IN THE RIGHT PLACE. Whether you'd like to optimize your day-to-day routines or you're considering a wholesale life change, you've found your compass.

You already possess the self-knowledge, passion, and experience to design the life you want. This weekly, 52-step workbook is your coach and companion as you reconnect with what you know at your core.

The techniques and prompts in these pages are rooted in appreciative inquiry, positive psychology, holistic coaching, and design thinking, spanning decades of research in the fields of personal development, life design, and time management. This workbook includes the most transformative exercises from my coaching practice – as well as the knowledge that comes with nearly 20 years of entrepreneurship, 5 decades of myriad life experience, the humbling awareness gained from birthing and raising 5 children, and a dogged commitment to learn from past choices that didn't yield the results I'd wanted as well as the choices that did.

The tools to design the life you want are here in your hands. You can't fail. The pace you set as you move through the workbook process is all yours: immerse yourself in this creative undertaking for an entire weekend or complete one exercise a week over the course of a year. Apart from the final section (which integrates your previous responses), navigate the pages chronologically or at random, as you prefer. When you complete the workbook, you'll know what you want your life to look like – and you'll have a plan to make it happen.

It's your life. Design it. Live it. Be you.

RESEARCH 7

1. APPRECIATIVE INQUIRY

WHAT'S WORKING WELL IN YOUR LIFE RIGHT NOW? List five things you feel good about. These can be major or seemingly mundane – it's up to you. Ideas: Positive habits you've successfully internalized (such as regularly getting more sleep, eating a plant-based diet, or disconnecting from e-mail at night); an amazing partner; a great new apartment; attending a writers' group; a religious or spiritual practice; a good relationship with your boss. Why are these elements affirmative? What are the positive impacts of the things on your list?

THINGS THAT ARE WORKING WELL	POSITIVE IMPACT
1.	
2.	
3.	
4.	
5.	

2. ABRACADABRA

IF YOU COULD WAVE A MAGIC WAND and change five things about your life today, what would they be? If you don't in fact own a magic wand, what is one thing you could do to improve each of these areas?

THINGS I'D LIKE TO CHANGE	FIRST STEP TOWARD IMPROVEMENT
1.	
2.	
3.	
4.	
5.	

IF YOU'RE TOTALLY STUCK with the second column, write down the name of a person or resource you can connect to for help.

3. NICE TO MEET YOU

YOU'RE AT A PARTY CHATTING WITH SOMEONE YOU'VE JUST MET.
How do you answer the inevitable question: "So, what do YOU do?"

WHEN YOU ANSWER THAT QUESTION, DO YOU FEEL SELF-CONFIDENT OR SELF-CONSCIOUS? Do you identify with a professional label? If you feel compelled to justify your life circumstance, why is that?

IF YOU AREN'T HAPPY ABOUT YOUR RESPONSE TO THE "WHAT DO YOU DO?" QUESTION, TRY CREATING A BETTER ELEVATOR SPEECH. Use this space to reframe what you do in a way that makes you stand with more confidence:

4. PASSION FRUIT

WHAT ARE YOU PASSIONATE ABOUT? What do you love? What are you willing to fight for? What fills you with energy or delight?

_____

_____

_____

_____

_____

_____

Don't loaf
and invite
inspiration;
LIGHT OUT AFTER
IT WITH A CLUB

Jack London

5. MIND THE GAP

WHAT'S MISSING FROM YOUR LIFE RIGHT NOW? Where do you feel depleted? Do you need more fun? More sleep? More love? More money? A job you feel good about? A reliable babysitter? A life purpose? Make a list of the absences or shortages that are important.

1. _____
2. _____
3. _____
4. _____
5. _____
6. _____
7. _____
8. _____
9. _____
10. _____
11. _____
12. _____
13. _____
14. _____
15. _____

NOTE BELOW THE THREE ABSENCES OR SHORTAGES THAT FEEL MOST SIGNIFICANT.

For each starred item, write one thing you can do this week to start filling in the gaps. Be creative – and just say "no thanks" to the voice that says you can't.

☆ _____

☆ _____

☆ _____

It matters
NOT HOW LONG
we live,
BUT HOW.

Philip James Bailey

6. REMEMBER WHEN

DURING CHILDHOOD, WHEN WERE YOU AT YOUR HAPPIEST?
What three events do you remember most fondly? Describe them here.

1. _____

_____

_____

2. _____

_____

_____

3. _____

_____

_____

WHAT WAS IT ABOUT THESE POSITIVE MEMORIES THAT STAYS WITH YOU?
How can you recapture or recreate some of those feelings in your life today?

_____

_____

_____

_____

7. TELL IT LIKE IT IS

WHAT ARE YOU GOOD AT? Brainstorm every talent you have, large and small. Think of every time someone said, "WOW, YOU'RE REALLY GOOD AT THAT!" Don't hold back.

WHAT HAVE YOU BEEN TRAINED TO DO?

WHAT HAVE YOU STUDIED ON YOUR OWN?

WHAT ARE YOUR TALENTS AND APTITUDES?

IN WHAT AREAS ARE YOU AN EXPERT?

After you've made your list, use markers or colored pens to draw connections between related items. What common threads or themes do you see here?

8. HIGHLIGHTS REEL

WHAT DO YOU CONSIDER YOUR FIVE GREATEST ACHIEVEMENTS THUS FAR?

Why? How do you feel about these accomplishments now? If any of these accomplishments were a team effort, who else was involved?

1. _____
2. _____
3. _____
4. _____
5. _____

WHICH ACHIEVEMENTS STIR THE MOST POSITIVE EMOTIONS?

_____
_____
_____
_____
_____

OTHERS INVOLVED

_____

_____

_____

HOW CAN YOU REPLICATE THESE SUCCESSES IN YOUR FUTURE? What do these past successes have in common?

_____

_____

_____

_____

_____

_____

_____

_____

_____

_____

9. THANKS, I NEEDED THAT

LOOKING BACK OVER THE PAST YEAR OR TWO, WHAT FIVE THINGS DO YOU FEEL MOST GRATEFUL FOR? A person, a gift, a practice, your career, a trip, a change in perspective?

1. _____

2. _____

3. _____

4. _____

5. _____

WHAT DID YOU LEARN DURING THIS TIME PERIOD?

_____

_____

_____

_____

_____

_____

_____

_____

_____

_____

Every truth we
see is ours to
give the world,
NOT TO KEEP
FOR OURSELVES
ALONE

Elizabeth Cady Stanton

10. CLEAN-UP IN AISLE THREE

FROM YOUR EARLIEST MEMORY UNTIL TODAY, what were your five biggest mistakes, screw-ups, lapses in judgement? Who was impacted?

CAN I GET A DO-OVER?	WHO WAS IMPACTED?
1.	
2.	
3.	
4.	
5.	

WHAT COULD YOU HAVE DONE DIFFERENTLY? What did you learn?

ARE THERE ANY COMMON THREADS AMONG YOUR ENTRIES?

11. BETTER THAN SPIN

LEARN TO REFRAME FAILURE OR REJECTION INTO AFFIRMATION

of your badassery. In life design, you can't fail. You try new things: if you like them, great; if you don't, you've been enriched by useful information and can move ahead all the wiser.

FOR EXAMPLE, HAVING YOUR NOVEL (or other creative work) rejected can be reframed as something positive. Here's how: "I had the courage to send my work into the world. I sent my work into the world because I believe it has value. I created that value by sitting at my desk (or easel or studio bench) and doing the work required. I could not have received this rejection if I had not in fact done the work and sent it out. Publishing is a numbers game; I will continue to send my work out and give myself credit for having the bravery to commit to my creative work."

PERCEPTION HAS A SYSTEMIC INFLUENCE on how you feel and the choices you make. Reframing past "failures" or rejections moves your focus back to process—and increases your productivity.

REFRAME FIVE "FAILURES" OR "REJECTIONS" HERE. Use the set you created in the previous exercise or any others you'd like to work through.

FAILURES	REFRAMES
1.	
2.	
3.	
4.	
5.	

12. A PERSON OF MANY HATS

WHAT DIFFERENT HATS DO YOU WEAR? Your role inventory might look something like: "Graphic designer, mother, partner to Chris, domestic goddess, shelter volunteer" – or it might look quite different. Limit yourself to 5-7 roles; if you have more than that, consolidate similar roles into broader categories.

ARE ANY OF THESE ROLES A HAT YOU NO LONGER WANT TO WEAR? If yes, what and why? Can you take that hat off?

13. IF I'M BEING HONEST

WHICH FIVE ASPECTS OF YOUR CHARACTER DO YOU LIKE THE MOST?
Are you empathetic, responsible, creative?

POSITIVE CHARACTER TRAITS:

1.

2.

3.

4.

5.

WHICH FIVE WOULD YOU LIKE TO CHANGE? Are you judgmental, impatient, pessimistic? Describe how you can address these or change them into positive attributes:

NOT-SO-GREAT CHARACTER TRAITS: CHANGE STRATEGIES

1. _____   _____

2. _____   _____

3. _____   _____

4. _____   _____

5. _____   _____

14. TREASURE TROVE

YOUR VALUES ARE THE UNDERPINNING OF EVERY CHOICE YOU MAKE.

Consider this values menu and circle the ten values you feel are most important. (If anything you value is missing, add it to the list.) Then, in a different color, circle the three values that are most essential to who you are.

AUTHENTICITY	COMMITMENT	COURAGE
CREATIVITY	CURIOSITY	DETERMINATION
EMPATHY	STRENGTH	EXCELLENCE
FAIRNESS	FAITH	GENEROSITY
GRACE	GROWTH	HAPPINESS
HONESTY	HUMOR	IMAGINATION
INDIVIDUALITY	INTEGRITY	JOY
JUSTICE	KINDNESS	LOVE
LOYALTY	OPENNESS	OPTIMISM
PEACE	PERSEVERANCE	
RESPECT	RESPONSIBILITY	
SELF-RELIANCE	SENSUALITY	

ARE YOU LIVING IN ACCORDANCE WITH YOUR THREE MOST ESSENTIAL VALUES?

If not, what changes do you need to make?

DAY BY DAY,
what you choose,
WHAT YOU THINK,
and what you do
IS WHO YOU BECOME.

Heraclitus

15. LOOKING UP

WHO ARE YOUR ROLE MODELS AND WHY? What traits do these individuals possess that you aspire to?

ROLE MODELS   TRAITS YOU ADMIRE

1. _____   _____

2. _____   _____

3. _____   _____

4. _____   _____

5. _____   _____

SEARCH FOR IMAGES of your three favorite role models and print one of each. Tape these images to your mirror. Every time you brush your teeth, remind yourself of these role models' traits and why their examples resonate with you. Determine to live according to your highest values, today and every day.

16. BODY OF WORK

HOW ARE YOU FEELING? Consider the Wellness Wheel below. Working from the middle of the circle to the outer edge, shade each wedge to reflect your assessment: if you're at your ideal weight, shade that wedge completely. If you're chronically sleep deprived, fill in just a tiny portion of the sleep wedge.

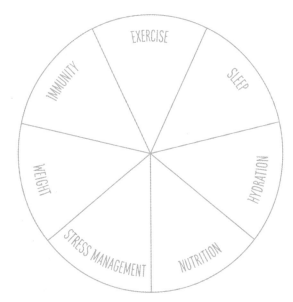

WHICH AREAS ARE MOST IN NEED OF ATTENTION? In which area would a change yield the most impact with the least effort? What would that change, or those changes, look like?

17. CITIZEN OF THE WORLD

WHAT ARE YOU CURIOUS ABOUT? List ten things you'd like to study or research. What do you need to do to explore these areas of interest: read books; take a class; join a group; take a trip? Lean toward exploration that takes you away from your computer and mobile phone.

THINGS THAT INTEREST ME	WAYS TO EXPLORE THEM
1.	
2.	
3.	
4.	
5.	
6.	
7.	
8.	
9.	
10.	

WHICH TOPIC ABOVE DO YOU WANT TO LEARN ABOUT FIRST?
Consider adding this adventure to your calendar on a specific date.

Date:

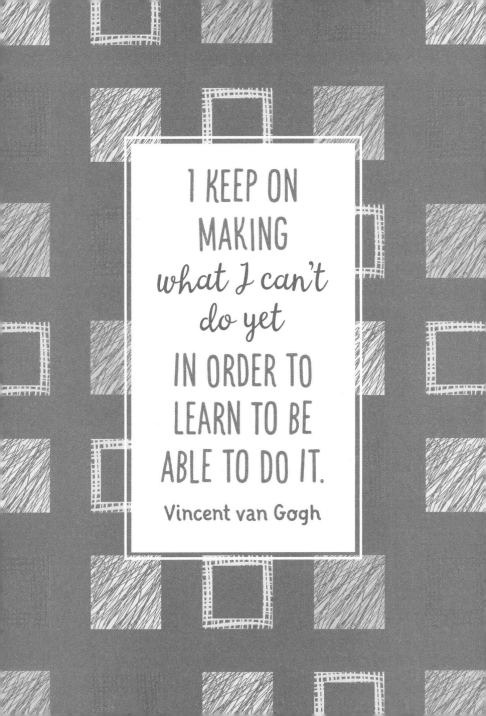

I KEEP ON
MAKING
*what I can't
do yet*
IN ORDER TO
LEARN TO BE
ABLE TO DO IT.

Vincent van Gogh

18. MIRROR, MIRROR, ON THE WALL

WHAT DO YOU LIKE MOST ABOUT YOUR APPEARANCE? What do you consider your best physical attributes?

WHAT MESSAGES ABOUT YOUR APPEARANCE DID YOU RECEIVE DURING CHILDHOOD? Do those messages impact you today?

DESCRIBE YOUR WARDROBE AND PERSONAL STYLE:

DOES THIS REPRESENT WHO YOU ARE? If not, what would you like to change?

PLAN for
WARDROBE
change

19. WHEN I GROW UP

WHEN YOU WERE A CHILD, WHAT DID YOU DREAM OF BECOMING AS AN ADULT?

DID YOU PURSUE ANY OF THOSE YOUTHFUL DREAMS? If you had areas of interest that faded as you grew older, why did that happen? Did you outgrow those dreams, deny them, or simply discover others?

HOW DO YOU ENJOY FREE TIME? How do you play? What makes you laugh? How do you define "fun"?

20. WORK HARD, PLAY HARD

TOO OFTEN, WE SPEND OUR NON-WORK HOURS engaged in activities that distract us without being restorative. What activities and people can you engage with for high-value recreation that fills the well?

ACTIVITIES THAT RESTORE ME:

PEOPLE WHO RESTORE ME:

21. THE HERO'S JOURNEY

WHAT SCARES YOU? How much do these fears hold you back?

WHAT CHALLENGES YOU? What is the bravest thing you've ever done?

WHEN DO YOU EXPERIENCE DEEP CONCENTRATION (FLOW)?

WHAT THREE THINGS WOULD YOU LIKE TO DO IF YOU KNEW YOU COULD NOT FAIL?

1.
2.
3.

22. ONCE UPON A TIME

AS HUMANS, WE'RE WIRED FOR STORY. Anthropologists have long since established that storytelling is essential to every known culture on Earth. Our DNA makes us experts in seeing narrative patterns and archetypes – which we use reflexively and subconsciously to make sense of the world and each other.

WHAT'S YOUR PERSONAL NARRATIVE? Use this space to write a third-person tale about your childhood, your life thus far, the life you'd like to have, or a hard-won insight.

23. HOME SWEET HOME

WHAT'S GREAT ABOUT THE CITY OR TOWN IN WHICH YOU LIVE?

WHAT DO YOU LIKE ABOUT YOUR HOUSE, APARTMENT, OR ROOM? How long do you plan to stay living where you are?

IN WHAT WAYS DOES YOUR HOME REFLECT YOUR PERSONALITY?

OF ALL THE PLACES YOU'VE EVER LIVED IN, WHICH DID YOU LIKE BEST—AND WHY?

WHAT THREE THINGS CAN YOU DO TO IMPROVE YOUR PERSONAL ENVIRONMENT?

1.
2.
3.

24. POSSESSED

OF ALL THE THINGS YOU OWN, WHAT FIVE ITEMS—OR CATEGORY OF ITEMS—DO YOU CARE ABOUT MOST? List them here. Next to each item, write what it symbolizes to you.

	PRIZED POSSESSIONS	WHAT THEY SYMBOLIZE
1.		
2.		
3.		
4.		
5.		

DO YOU MAINTAIN ANY COLLECTIONS, EITHER INTENTIONALLY OR BY ACCIDENT? WHAT ARE THEY?

DO YOU HAVE TOO MANY THINGS, OR NOT ENOUGH? ARE YOUR POSSESSIONS ENHANCING YOUR LIFE, OR WEIGHING YOU DOWN?

_____

_____

_____

_____

IF YOU NEED TO IMPROVE THE WAY YOU MANAGE YOUR BELONGINGS, WHAT WOULD YOU LIKE TO CHANGE? List five areas of your home that you'd like to work on:

1. _____

2. _____

3. _____

4. _____

5. _____

WE MUST BELIEVE
THAT WE ARE GIFTED
for something and
THAT THIS THING,
at whatever cost,
MUST BE ATTAINED.

Marie Curie

25. IT DOESN'T GROW ON TREES

IN SPECIFIC TERMS, WHAT ARE YOUR FINANCIAL GOALS?
What are your assets? Do you feel secure about your current
and future financial picture?

WHAT FOUR ACTIONS COULD YOU TAKE TO MAINTAIN OR CREATE FINANCIAL
SECURITY? Write them below and then add them to your calendar.
*Consider items that also create security for your children and other family
members, such as college savings or a will.

1.

2.

3.

4.

STRATEGY

55

26. TIME'S A WASTIN'

WHAT ARE YOUR BIGGEST TIME SINKS? What activities ultimately make you feel like you've wasted your time? These might be things you don't want to do but "have to," or things like watching TV, getting sucked into Facebook or Reddit, playing the latest addictive game on your smartphone, or shopping (online or in person).

ON AVERAGE, HOW MUCH TIME PER DAY DO YOU SPEND DOING THE THINGS ABOVE? Be real with yourself. Write that amount in the circle next to each activity below.

_____   hours

_____   hours

_____   hours

_____   hours

DOES THIS FEEL LIKE THE RIGHT AMOUNT OF TIME? Is there anything you'd like to change about your time investment in this area? List three ways in which you could manage your time differently to increase your happiness. What would you like to do with the time you'll gain as a result?

time **MANAGEMENT** *strategies*

1. _____

2. _____

3. _____

WHAT I'LL DO WITH MY ADDITIONAL FREE TIME:

_____

_____

_____

_____

_____

_____

_____

_____

_____

_____

_____

_____

_____

27. PRACTICE MAKES PERFECT

WHAT REGULAR HABITS, ROUTINES, OR PRACTICES would you like to develop over the next three months? Are there ways that you could improve your morning and evening routines to better support your work and home life? Consider options such as: getting up 30 minutes earlier; cleaning the kitchen before going to bed; weekly planning; batch cooking; random acts of kindness; a daily walk before lunch; meditating; making the bed; praying.

PLAN for
ADDING
new
routines

PURSUITS BECOME HABITS.

Ovid

28. THE GREAT EQUALIZER

EACH ONE OF US—NO MATTER WHO WE ARE, where we live, how much money we make—gets 168 hours every week. When we spend those hours, we can't get them back. Let's determine exactly how much of your time is spoken for and then calculate how much "discretionary" time is left over. Here's an example:

LOUISE'S ACTIVITIES	HOURS DAILY	DAYS PER WEEK	HOURS WEEKLY
Sleeping	8	7	56
Working (excluding weekends)	9	5	45
Commuting (excluding weekends)	1	5	5
Eating	.75	7	5.25
Personal hygiene	.5	7	3.5
Exercising	.5	7	3.5
Domestics: cooking, cleaning, laundry, shopping, errands	1.5	7	10.5
Family caretaking	1.5	7	7
HOURS SPOKEN FOR EACH WEEK:			135.75
TIME LEFT OVER EACH WEEK:			32.25

IN THIS EXAMPLE, Louise works full time, commutes, exercises, takes care of her family and home, sleeps 8 hours a night, and still has more than 30 hours a week left over for recreation, side projects, and spending time with family and friends.

NOW, LET'S THINK ABOUT YOUR 168 HOURS. If you aren't sure where your time goes each week, keep a log. Then complete the chart below, adding in the activities that occupy your week.

ACTIVITY	HOURS DAILY	DAYS PER WEEK	HOURS WEEKLY
Sleeping			
Working			
Commuting			
Eating			
Personal hygiene			
HOURS SPOKEN FOR EACH WEEK:			
TIME LEFT OVER EACH WEEK:			

ANALYZE. Are you spending your hours the way you want? Does your schedule reflect your values and priorities? What changes do you want to make? What three things will you do to make those changes?

_____

_____

_____

FOREVER—IS
composed
OF NOWS—

Emily Dickinson

29. AT THE VERY LEAST

WHAT'S ESSENTIAL TO YOUR WELL-BEING ON A DAILY BASIS? Do you
notice a difference when you take your vitamin supplements, drink two
liters of water, listen to music, take a brisk walk, meditate, eat fresh
vegetables, and get the right amount of sleep? List your essentials and
commit to doing all of them every day.

THINGS THAT ARE ESSENTIAL TO MY WELL-BEING

1. _____
2. _____
3. _____
4. _____
5. _____
6. _____
7. _____
8. _____
9. _____
10. _____

THESE ARE YOUR MINIMUM DAILY REQUIREMENTS. Photocopy or rewrite your
list on an index card and stick it to your bathroom mirror or fridge.

30. CUT THAT OUT

WHAT ARE YOUR NOT-SO-GREAT HABITS OR PATTERNS? What would you like to let go? Do you find yourself avoiding important work, eating too much sugar, hitting the snooze button three times every morning, staring at your phone instead of engaging with the world around you? What about things that are harder to see in oneself, such as interrupting instead of listening, jumping to conclusions, or negative self-talk? List five patterns you could eliminate right now to your benefit and a strategy for leaving each one on the cutting-room floor.

NOT SO GREAT HABITS   ELIMINATION STRATEGY

1.

2.

3.

4.

5.

THE ONLY PERSON
you are destined
TO BECOME
is the person
YOU DECIDE TO BE.

Ralph Waldo Emerson

The beginning
IS ALWAYS TODAY.

Mary Wollstonecraft

31. SUDDEN OPPORTUNITIES

WHEN YOU FIND YOURSELF WITH A FEW SPARE MINUTES—WAITING

at the doctor's office, sitting in your car, or waiting for the pasta pot to boil—take advantage of the opportunity to do a few things that restore you and are aligned with your values and interests, as opposed to reflexively picking up your phone. To get started, make a list of things you can do or enjoy for 5 to 30 minutes. For example, stretch out, work on a crossword puzzle, water your flowers, or write a poem. Your list:

1. _____

2. _____

3. _____

4. _____

5. _____

6. _____

7. _____

8. _____

9. _____

10. _____

32. WHO'S ON MY TEAM?

USE THE THREE CONCENTRIC CIRCLES below to identify your team.
You are in the center circle.

me

Within the next circle, write the names of the people who are closest to you. These are the people who you trust to lend you support.

IN THE OUTER CIRCLE, list the people who aren't in the inner circle, but still provide support (even if you aren't in regular contact). In either ring, you might also include groups or communities that fall within your support network.

GIVEN THAT RELATIONSHIPS EVOLVE OVER TIME, people may move back and forth between the inner and outer circles. What looks right today may look different next month.

SUMMARIZE ANY DISCOVERIES, AFFIRMATIONS, OR AREAS WHERE YOU MAY NEED TO DEVELOP MORE SUPPORT. For a more detailed analysis, create different versions for your personal life, professional life, and so on. Repeat this process occasionally to take stock of your support network.

PLAN *for*
DEVELOPING
support

33. BIRDS OF A FEATHER

WHAT AND WHOM DO YOU RELY ON FOR INSPIRATION, CONNECTION, AND ACCOUNTABILITY? Are the rings in your "Who's on My Team" exercise a little sparse? Is it time to reconnect with friends and associates from the past? Data shows that emotions and behaviors are both contagious, so it's vital to hang out with people who inspire positive emotions and behaviors that support your goals. Let's work on your affinity group repertoire:

JOIN COMMUNITIES

NICHE GROUPS EXIST on most social media platforms and across the internet. Hunt for online communities and join or bookmark the ones you like. Earn a "gold star" if you join 10 or more. (Liking a Facebook page doesn't count. Joining a Facebook group does.) Write group names here:

1.
2.
3.
4.
5.
6.
7.
8.
9.
10.

FIND OPPORTUNITIES TO CONNECT

USE YOUR GOOGLE–FU to identify resources in your area where you might make connections. (Being an introvert doesn't get you off the hook here, by the way.) Subscribe to local newsletters. Look for an interesting upcoming event or class and sign up. Write resource names here:

IDENTIFY MENTORS:

LOOKING BACK TO YOUR EARLIEST DAYS, who are the people that believed in you? Which relatives, friends, teachers, coaches, caregivers, co-workers, and neighbors saw and encouraged your talent and potential? How did these individuals communicate their support? What impact did this support have on you – then, and today?

WHAT MIGHT YOU DO TO CONNECT WITH YOUR TRIBE MORE OFTEN, either in person or online? Write a plan to build connections with the communities that resonate. Then pick one of your connection tasks, and do it. Right now. Record your plan here:

PLAN *for* **BUILDING** *connections*

34. LOVE STORY

WHO—OR WHAT—IS THE GREATEST LOVE OF YOUR LIFE? How has this love changed you?

IS THIS LOVE PART OF YOUR PAST AND/OR PRESENT? Is this love part of your vision for the future?

LIST FIVE WAYS IN WHICH YOU MIGHT BETTER ENGAGE with a current love, celebrate a past love, or create the future love relationship you want.

1. _____

2. _____

3. _____

4. _____

5. _____

DEVELOPMENT 77

35. MAKING A MARK

UP UNTIL NOW, WHAT HAS BEEN YOUR LIFE'S WORK?

DO YOU CONSIDER THIS AREA OF FOCUS TO BE YOUR CALLING? Do you want to make a change in this commitment? Why or why not?

36. DREAM BIG

IF YOU WON THE LOTTERY TOMORROW and no longer had to think about your income, how would you spend your time? Would you continue doing the work you're doing now – or do something completely different?

ARE THERE ANY ELEMENTS of your lottery-winning scenario that you can start working toward even without a windfall? Describe those elements here and how you would work toward them.

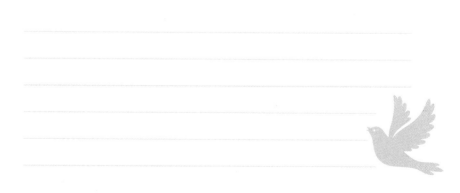

37. BE THE CHANGE

HOW DO YOU WANT TO MAKE THE WORLD A BETTER PLACE? What non-governmental organizations do you support, or would you like to support, with time or money?

WHAT FIVE SOCIAL ISSUES OR HUMANITARIAN CONCERNS TOP YOUR LIST?
Write them here:

1.
2.
3.
4.
5.

ARE THESE FIVE ISSUES ABOVE CONNECTED TO YOUR LIFE'S WORK? Does your level of philanthropic involvement feel right – or does it merit adjustment?

38. YOUR DREAM DAY

WHAT DOES YOUR IDEAL DAY LOOK LIKE, FROM START TO FINISH?

Be as descriptive as possible. For example: "I wake up refreshed after a solid night's sleep. After snuggling with my significant other, I go downstairs to make tea. I am grateful for my tidy, organized home. I feed the dog and sit at the table to eat a healthy breakfast while I read the paper for 15 minutes. Then I....."

WORKDAY DREAM DAY:

WEEKEND DREAM DAY:

ABOVE ALL THINGS,
never think that
you're not good
enough yourself.

Anthony Trollope

39. OH, WHAT A YEAR IT WAS

CREATE A JOURNAL ENTRY DATED ONE YEAR FROM NOW. Writing in the first person, detail your successes of the past year. Describe the things that pleased you, and explain why they happened. Note the practices and new habits you developed or changed, the things you accomplished, and the ways in which you grew as a person. What dreams did you accomplish – and how?

Date one year from today

40. THE BUCKET LIST

TWENTY-FIVE THINGS TO DO BEFORE YOU DIE. GO.

1.
2.
3.
4.
5.
6.
7.
8.
9.
10.
11.
12.
13.
14.
15.
16.
17.

18. _____
19. _____
20. _____
21. _____
22. _____
23. _____
24. _____
25. _____

SELECT ONE OF THESE ITEMS TO DO WITHIN THE NEXT SIX MONTHS. What's your plan for making this happen?

_____

_____

_____

_____

_____

_____

_____

_____

41. LOOKING AHEAD

WHAT DO YOU WANT YOUR LIFE TO LOOK LIKE IN THE NEXT THREE YEARS? What milestones do you want to have accomplished? How does this future life differ from the life you're living today?

ENVISIONING
The next **3** YEARS

FILL IN GOALS, INTENTIONS, OR IDEAS that feel right for each period of time. Don't worry if there's repetition among timeframes. Think big, think small. Try not to censor yourself too much; remember, these are just possibilities. You aren't committing to anything here.

MY LIFE IN ONE YEAR

_____

_____

_____

_____

_____

_____

_____

MY LIFE IN SIX MONTHS

_____

_____

_____

_____

_____

_____

42. IF/THEN

HOW WILL YOU FEEL WHEN YOU'RE LIVING THE LIFE YOU WANT?

How are those feelings different from what you feel now?

FAILURE
IS
IMPOSSIBLE.

Susan B. Anthony

43. LIVING LARGE

WHAT ARE THREE THINGS THAT HOLD YOU BACK FROM ACCOMPLISHING YOUR WILDEST DREAMS?

1. _____
2. _____
3. _____

WHAT IS IT COSTING YOU TO HOLD BACK?

_____
_____
_____
_____
_____
_____
_____
_____
_____
_____

CHOOSE ONE IMPEDIMENT THAT YOU CAN OVERCOME AND WRITE YOUR ACTION
PLAN HERE.

PLAN *for*
OVERCOMING
an
OBSTACLE

44. SOAP BOX

WHAT IS THE PURPOSE OF LIFE?

WHAT IS THE PURPOSE OF WORK?

ADD YOUR ANSWERS TO THE VENN DIAGRAM BELOW FOR COMPARISON. If you find common elements where these paradigms intersect, write those in the "sweet spot" in the center of the diagram.

PURPOSE OF WORK

SWEET SPOT

PURPOSE OF LIFE

WHAT YOU LEAVE BEHIND
is not what is
ENGRAVED IN
stone monuments,
BUT WHAT IS WOVEN
into the lives
OF OTHERS.

Pericles

45. MY LEGACY

IN LIFE DESIGN, IT'S ESSENTIAL TO BEGIN WITH THE END IN MIND.

So let's jump to the very end. Write the obituary you hope to one day merit. How do you want to be remembered? What kind of legacy do you want to leave behind? What do you want your loved ones to remember about you?

46. LIFE PURPOSE

IRONY NOTWITHSTANDING, LET'S DO A POST-MORTEM on the obituary you wrote in the last exercise. When you take your last few breaths, are you going to think back gratefully on all the e-mails you answered, the evenings you spent watching TV you didn't care about, hours spent playing Words with Friends, or sleep lost to anxiety? Highlight the elements in your obituary that are most actionable. Use that starting place to draft your life purpose statement.

MY LIFE PURPOSE IS TO:

KEEP AWAY FROM PEOPLE
who try to belittle
YOUR AMBITIONS.
Small people always
DO THAT, BUT THE REALLY
great ones make you
FEEL THAT YOU TOO
can become great.

Mark Twain

PRODUCTION

101

47. TREE OF LIFE DESIGN: INHERITANCE

ALL THE AREAS WE'VE COVERED IN THIS WORKBOOK are key
components of your Tree of Life design.

BELOW THE GROUND'S SURFACE, your background and inherent proclivities
are the unseen base of your tree. This includes your history, genetics,
and predispositions. While these elements cannot be changed, it's critical
to understand how this foundation impacts your past, present, and
future.

You explored your inheritance in these exercises: REMEMBER WHEN; TELL
IT LIKE IT IS; HIGHLIGHTS REEL; THANKS, I NEEDED THAT; CLEAN-UP IN AISLE
THREE; IF I'M BEING HONEST; ONCE UPON A TIME.

AFTER READING YOUR RESPONSES TO THE ABOVE EXERCISES, list five positive
events, inherent attributes, or experiences from your childhood that
impact you today.

1. _____

2. _____

3. _____

4. _____

5. _____

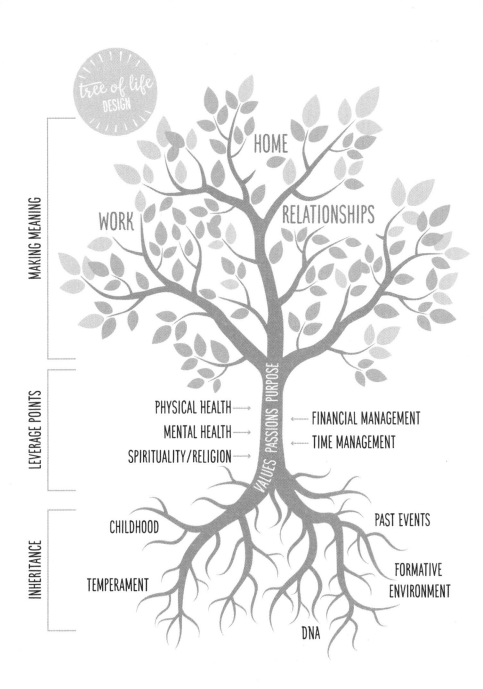

tree of life
DESIGN

MAKING MEANING

HOME

WORK

RELATIONSHIPS

LEVERAGE POINTS

VALUES PASSIONS PURPOSE

PHYSICAL HEALTH →

MENTAL HEALTH →

SPIRITUALITY/RELIGION →

← FINANCIAL MANAGEMENT

← TIME MANAGEMENT

INHERITANCE

CHILDHOOD

PAST EVENTS

TEMPERAMENT

FORMATIVE
ENVIRONMENT

DNA

WHAT IS THE POSITIVE IMPACT OF SOME OF THE ITEMS ON YOUR LIST?

How can you amplify these assets?

_____

_____

_____

_____

_____

LIST THREE CHALLENGING OR DIFFICULT EVENTS, INHERENT TRAITS, OR EXPERIENCES FROM YOUR CHILDHOOD THAT IMPACT YOU TODAY.

1. _____

2. _____

3. _____

WHAT IS THE ADVERSE IMPACT OF SOME OF THE ITEMS LISTED ABOVE?

How can you mitigate the lingering impact of this inventory? Could any of your entries be inverted and transformed into positive action?

_____

_____

_____

_____

_____

A person often
MEETS HIS DESTINY
on the road
HE TOOK TO
avoid it.
Jean de La Fontaine

48. TREE OF LIFE DESIGN: LEVERAGE POINTS

THE CHOICES YOU MAKE TODAY INFORM YOUR ULTIMATE OUTCOME,

and how much you enjoy the process while you're getting there.
(Many would argue that the journey is at least as important as the
destination.) Physical health, mental health, spirituality/religion, financial
management, and time management are all aspects of your life that
you can at least in part regulate. While you can't necessarily control or
avoid disease, accidents, or an economic crash, you have the power to
use these leverage points to support your life's purpose.

You explored your leverage points in these exercises: APPRECIATIVE
INQUIRY; ABRACADABRA; MIND THE GAP; BETTER THAN SPIN; BODY OF WORK;
MIRROR, MIRROR, ON THE WALL; HOME SWEET HOME; POSSESSED; IT DOESN'T
GROW ON TREES; TIME'S A WASTIN'; PRACTICE MAKES PERFECT; THE GREAT
EQUALIZER; AT THE VERY LEAST; CUT THAT OUT; SUDDEN OPPORTUNITIES;
LIVING LARGE.

THE UPWARD MOTION IN YOUR TREE comes from your values, passions, and
life purpose. These form the tireless trunk of your tree. These are your
guiding principles; your mission.

You explored the trunk of your tree in these exercises: NICE TO MEET YOU;
PASSION FRUIT; TREASURE TROVE; LOOKING UP; CITIZEN OF THE WORLD; WHEN
I GROW UP; WORK HARD, PLAY HARD; THE HERO'S JOURNEY; MAKING A MARK;
DREAM BIG; BE THE CHANGE; YOUR DREAM DAY; OH, WHAT A YEAR IT WAS; THE
BUCKET LIST; LOOKING AHEAD; IF/THEN; SOAP BOX; MY LEGACY; LIFE PURPOSE.

AFTER READING YOUR RESPONSES IN THE LEVERAGE-POINTS EXERCISES, ANSWER THE FOLLOWING QUESTIONS:

WHAT DO YOU WANT MOST IN THE SCOPE OF PHYSICAL HEALTH? Why does this matter?

WHAT DO YOU WANT MOST IN THE SPHERE OF MENTAL AND EMOTIONAL HEALTH? Why does this matter?

WHAT DO YOU WANT MOST IN THE REALM OF SPIRITUALITY OR RELIGION?
Why does this matter?

_____

_____

_____

_____

_____

_____

_____

WHAT DO YOU WANT YOUR FINANCIAL PICTURE TO LOOK LIKE? Why does
this matter?

_____

_____

_____

_____

_____

_____

_____

WHAT DO YOU WANT YOUR TIME-MANAGEMENT PRACTICES TO LOOK LIKE?

Why does this matter?

49. TREE OF LIFE DESIGN: MAKING MEANING

ULTIMATELY, THE ROLES YOU IDENTIFIED on page 28 are the meaning in your life; the leaves of your tree. These will be different for everyone, but in broad terms these areas are relationships, work, and home.

You explored how you make meaning in these exercises: A PERSON OF MANY HATS; WHO'S ON MY TEAM; BIRDS OF A FEATHER; LOVE STORY; TREE OF LIFE DESIGN: INHERITANCE; TREE OF LIFE DESIGN: LEVERAGE POINTS.

USING THE BROAD CATEGORIES of relationships, work, and home, what is your dream scenario in each of these areas? What would you like each of these leaves to look like in 10 years?

RELATIONSHIPS:

_____

_____

_____

_____

_____

_____

_____

WORK:

_____

_____

_____

_____

_____

_____

_____

_____

HOME:

_____

_____

_____

_____

_____

_____

_____

_____

PERFORM
WITHOUT FAIL
what you
RESOLVE.

Benjamin Franklin

50. YOUR MAP

YOU'VE EXPLORED, ASSESSED, CONNECTED, AND REFLECTED. It's time to make your life-design map and get on the road. What do you want to accomplish in the next 12 months? Be specific with your intentions; this exercise will become your navigation companion. Look carefully at what you wrote in the previous three exercises.

RELATIONSHIPS:

HOME:

WORK:

_____

_____

_____

_____

PHYSICAL HEALTH:

_____

_____

_____

_____

MENTAL/EMOTIONAL HEALTH:

_____

_____

_____

_____

SPIRITUALITY/RELIGION:

_____
_____
_____
_____

FINANCES:

_____
_____
_____
_____

TIME MANAGEMENT:

_____
_____
_____
_____

51. FROM DREAM TO REALITY

AS WE KNOW PAINFULLY WELL, a goal without a timeline is just a dream. Whether you schedule your time with Google Calendar, Filofax, Outlook, Moleskine, a spiral-bound notebook, or any of the many inspiring time-management tools available, committing to a trackable system is essential to meeting your goals. Choose your time-management system and write it here:

TAKE ONE OF YOUR LONGER-TERM GOALS AT A TIME and break it into actionable steps using the SMART Goal approach. Map out your goal milestones in the days, weeks, or months that follow using the SMART Goal Worksheets.

SMART GOAL WORKSHEET 🖉

SPECIFIC: What exactly do you want to accomplish? Precision and simplicity are powerful.

MEASURABLE: What are the concrete criteria by which you will measure your progress?

ATTAINABLE: An attainable goal encourages you to stretch, but does not set you up for failure.

RELEVANT: Is your goal relevant to your values, roles, passions, and purpose?

TIME-BASED: What is the timeframe within which you will accomplish this goal?

MY SPECIFIC, MEASURABLE GOAL IS:

_____

_____

I WILL KNOW I REACHED MY GOAL WHEN:

_____

_____

I KNOW THAT I CAN REACH THIS GOAL BECAUSE:

_____

_____

MY PERSONAL VALUES ASSOCIATED WITH THIS GOAL ARE:

_____

_____

MY DEADLINE OR TARGET DATE FOR COMPLETION IS:

_____

_____

[ ] I have added related tasks and milestones to my
personal calendar

SMART GOAL WORKSHEET ✏️

SPECIFIC: What exactly do you want to accomplish?
Precision and simplicity are powerful.

MEASURABLE: What are the concrete criteria by which you
will measure your progress?

ATTAINABLE: An attainable goal encourages you to stretch,
but does not set you up for failure.

RELEVANT: Is your goal relevant to your values, roles,
passions, and purpose?

TIME-BASED: What is the timeframe within which you will
accomplish this goal?

MY SPECIFIC, MEASURABLE GOAL IS:

_____

_____

I WILL KNOW I REACHED MY GOAL WHEN:

_____

_____

I KNOW THAT I CAN REACH THIS GOAL BECAUSE:

_____

_____

MY PERSONAL VALUES ASSOCIATED WITH THIS GOAL ARE:

_____

_____

MY DEADLINE OR TARGET DATE FOR COMPLETION IS:

_____

_____

[ ] I have added related tasks and milestones to my personal calendar

SMART GOAL WORKSHEET ✏️

SPECIFIC: What exactly do you want to accomplish? Precision and simplicity are powerful.

MEASURABLE: What are the concrete criteria by which you will measure your progress?

ATTAINABLE: An attainable goal encourages you to stretch, but does not set you up for failure.

RELEVANT: Is your goal relevant to your values, roles, passions, and purpose?

TIME-BASED: What is the timeframe within which you will accomplish this goal?

MY SPECIFIC, MEASURABLE GOAL IS:

_____

_____

I WILL KNOW I REACHED MY GOAL WHEN:

_____

_____

I KNOW THAT I CAN REACH THIS GOAL BECAUSE:

_____

_____

MY PERSONAL VALUES ASSOCIATED WITH THIS GOAL ARE:

_____

_____

MY DEADLINE OR TARGET DATE FOR COMPLETION IS:

_____

_____

[   ] I have added related tasks and milestones to my
personal calendar

SMART GOAL WORKSHEET 🖉

SPECIFIC: What exactly do you want to accomplish? Precision and simplicity are powerful.

MEASURABLE: What are the concrete criteria by which you will measure your progress?

ATTAINABLE: An attainable goal encourages you to stretch, but does not set you up for failure.

RELEVANT: Is your goal relevant to your values, roles, passions, and purpose?

TIME-BASED: What is the timeframe within which you will accomplish this goal?

MY SPECIFIC, MEASURABLE GOAL IS:

_____

_____

I WILL KNOW I REACHED MY GOAL WHEN:

_____

_____

I KNOW THAT I CAN REACH THIS GOAL BECAUSE:

_____

_____

MY PERSONAL VALUES ASSOCIATED WITH THIS GOAL ARE:

_____

_____

MY DEADLINE OR TARGET DATE FOR COMPLETION IS:

_____

_____

[ ] I have added related tasks and milestones to my
personal calendar

SMART GOAL WORKSHEET ✏️

SPECIFIC: What exactly do you want to accomplish? Precision and simplicity are powerful.

MEASURABLE: What are the concrete criteria by which you will measure your progress?

ATTAINABLE: An attainable goal encourages you to stretch, but does not set you up for failure.

RELEVANT: Is your goal relevant to your values, roles, passions, and purpose?

TIME-BASED: What is the timeframe within which you will accomplish this goal?

MY SPECIFIC, MEASURABLE GOAL IS:

_____

_____

I WILL KNOW I REACHED MY GOAL WHEN:

_____

_____

I KNOW THAT I CAN REACH THIS GOAL BECAUSE:

_____

_____

MY PERSONAL VALUES ASSOCIATED WITH THIS GOAL ARE:

_____

_____

MY DEADLINE OR TARGET DATE FOR COMPLETION IS:

_____

_____

[ ] I have added related tasks and milestones to my
personal calendar

52. ACCOUNTABILITY TOOLS

NOW THAT YOU'RE SET UP, what will you do to interact with your system on a daily basis and stay on track? Set aside 15 minutes every Sunday to plan the coming week.

WHAT OTHER ACCOUNTABILITY TOOLS CAN YOU ADD TO YOUR SYSTEM?

CONGRATULATIONS. You've reached the end of this workbook. Your personal compass is securely in the palm of your hand. The time is now: Live your one wild and precious life as only you can. Bravo!

MIRANDA HERSEY is a writer, editor, and certified creativity coach. Her work has appeared in *The Boston Globe, Boston Globe Magazine, Sun Magazine,* and *Bay Area Parent,* among other publications. A dual national of Britain and the U.S.—and mother of five—Miranda is living her dream in Bainbridge Island, Washington.